Eas[y-to-Build] Adirondack [Furniture]

Mary Twitchell

CONTENTS

Introduction

Building Adirondack furniture is a time-honored craft. Sturdy and rustic, this furniture can be a beautiful addition to any indoor decor, although it's most often used to set the scene outdoors. There, the furniture is subjected to a lifetime of abuse. Yearly it moves from somewhere hidden away (probably dark and musty winter storage) to front-and-center on the summer stage. Now, hour after hour it is beaten on by intense UV light, drenched in driving rains, then fried again in the summer sun. Through it all, the furniture patiently endures — ever handsome, ever inviting, ever lasting. To survive summertime abuse and the semiannual ritual of being dragged into and out of storage, outdoor furniture must be sturdy, rugged, and well built — all qualities that epitomize Adirondack pieces.

This bulletin contains instructions for building an Adirondack chair, matching footstool, companion side table, and Westport chair (an ancestor of the modern-day slatted Adirondack chair). Each project will take the moderately skilled carpenter less than a day to fabricate; for the beginner, maybe a weekend. However, none of the cuts is difficult, and no special tools are required.

Choosing the Right Lumber

When furniture is set outdoors, its wood is exposed to wet weather, damp soils, and insects — all the conditions that stress joints and cause wood to rot. Naturally decay-resistant woods such as western red cedar, cypress, redwood, and white oak are therefore the smartest building materials. These species, however, are expensive; Douglas fir and southern yellow pine are less decay resistant but when painted they make attractive and durable substitutes.

Pressure-treated lumber will last for 20 years (much longer than untreated woods). There were multiple health concerns related to the older CCA treated lumber, but today's versions are safer. You may also object to putting your skin in constant contact with chemically treated wood. A compromise solution is to cut your chair's legs and stringers (they come in contact with the ground and are therefore the most susceptible to rot) out of pressure-treated lumber, then construct the rest of the piece from untreated stock.

Regardless of wood species, choose your lumber carefully. Avoid boards that cup, twist, or bow. They will make construction much more difficult, if not impossible. Choose boards with as few knots as possible. Sometimes you can avoid the knots by judicious cutting, other times not. Before final placement of any precut piece, check the two surfaces and place the better surface face up.

Fasteners

When considering what type of screws to use, focus on the galvanized, brass, stainless-steel, or zinc-coated varieties. Stainless-steel drywall screws with a Phillips head are easily driven by a power drill fitted with a Phillips-head driver. These screws won't corrode or rust, but they are expensive.

For strength and a sense of aesthetics, choose straight, sturdy boards with as few knots as possible.

Bits used to drill pilot holes should be of the same diameter as the solid part of the screw (that is, minus the threads). Drill pilot holes for all screws. If a screw is countersunk close to a board's edge, the wood is likely to split; predrilling the holes prevents this. Should the wood split, turn over the board or cut a replacement piece.

If the screws will show on your final piece, pay close attention to their placement. Screw heads should create a consistent pattern. For the slats, inset the screws ⅜" (1 cm) from the sawed ends and use two screws per end.

Whenever larger surfaces adjoin (stringers to legs, for example), use three screws in a triangular or diagonal pattern so that the screws enter the wood in different grains. For greater strength, screw from both sides of a joint.

Glue

Use a waterproof carpenter's wood glue; this is yellowish, and it will strengthen wood joints. Apply glue to adjoining surfaces. If you've applied too much, it will ooze out the edges when the boards are screwed together. With a wet rag, remove the excess before it dries. If it is allowed to dry, the excess glue will have to be chipped off and will leave a stain on the wood.

Finding a Construction Surface

For Adirondack furniture assembly, work on a smooth and level surface; otherwise the pieces won't sit squarely when finished. If you're building on your garage floor, for instance, check first whether its floor slopes toward a floor drain.

Sanding

The directions here call for sanding the pieces after they've been cut but before they are assembled; because of the slat construction, it is very difficult to sand the wood once the chair has been screwed together. Sand first with a medium grit paper (120 grit), then with a fine grit (220).

A 1" x 3" x 4" (2.5 x 7.6 x 10.1 cm) sanding block wrapped with sandpaper is easy to use if you're hand-sanding; a palm sander, random orbital sander, or belt sander will make the process quicker.

Finishing Tips

The finish you choose may depend in part on which wood you choose. For decay-resistant woods (redwood, cedar, cypress, oak), use exterior stains and varnishes; they let the natural grain of the wood show through. Softwoods (pine, fir) have knots and imperfections, which will look better if painted.

Wood sealers maintain the wood's natural appearance. Apply three coats with a brush or roller. Wait until the previous coat has dried before applying the next.

Stains, on the other hand, impart a brown or gray color to the wood.

If you choose to paint your furniture, prime all surfaces before assembly. When the project has been completed, apply two coats of high-gloss or enamel paint. Dark green, gray, and white are the traditional colors, but the primary colors — red, blue, and yellow — are also becoming popular.

The Adirondack Chair

The Adirondack chair has graced lawns for more than 90 years. Originally called the Westport chair (it was designed by Thomas Lee for his home in Westport, New York), the chair has always been associated with life at the "great camps" (the summer residences of the Rockefellers, the Vanderbilts, and their peers) in the Adirondack Mountains of upper New York State.

The design of the chair is unique. With its five-slatted, sloped back, its wide arms, and its steeply angled seat, the Adirondack chair is instantly recognizable. Its design is simple, unfettered, and amazingly attractive with straight clean lines and an alluring low profile — a sharp contrast to its wobbly modern-day counterpart of molded plastic or twisted aluminum and frayed plastic webbing.

The Adirondack chair is a classic element of our rural landscapes. It is sturdy, simple, and attractive and will last many, many years.

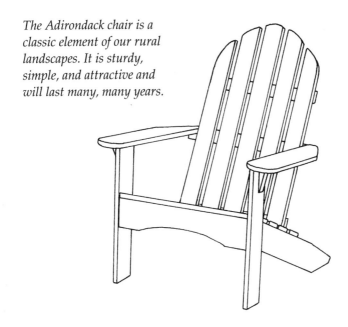

Materials and Tools for the Adirondack Chair

Tools

Tape measure

4' (1.2 m) level

Power drill with Phillips-head driver, or Phillips-head screwdriver

Drill bit for pilot holes

Circular saw or ripsaw

1" (2.5 cm) chisel

Rafter's square

Sanding block, palm sander, or belt sander with assortment of sandpaper (coarse to fine)

Framing or rafter's square

T-bevel

Hammer

Jigsaw

Handsaw

Pencil

Carpenter's wood glue

3' (91.1 cm) piece of string and compass

Fasteners

1 box of 2" and one box of 1¼" (4.1 cm) stainless-steel drywall screws, **or** #8 stainless-steel, brass, or galvanized wood screws (approximately 90 screws)

Lumber

3 10-foot (3 m) lengths of standard 1" x 4" lumber

1 6-foot (1.8 m) length of standard 1" x 4" lumber

1 8-foot (2.4 m) length of standard 1" x 6" lumber

1 6-foot (1.8 m) length of standard 1" x 6" lumber

Cutting List for the Adirondack Chair

Quantity	Use	Dimensions	Length of Pieces
2	front legs	1" x 4"	24" (60.7 cm)
1	arm supports	1" x 4"	6" (15.2 cm)
1	top back brace	1" x 4"	19½" (49.3 cm)
1	bottom back brace	1" x 4"	19½" (49.3 cm)
5	seat slats	1" x 4"	21" (53.1 cm)
5	back slats	1" x 4"	36" (91.1 cm)
1	back support	1" x 4"	21" (53.1 cm)
1	arm connector	1" x 4"	26" (65.8 cm)
2	stringers	1" x 6"	39½" (99.9 cm)
2	arms	1" x 6"	28½" (72.1 cm)
1	front brace	1" x 6"	21" (53.1 cm)

1. Cut the pieces. Cut the lumber as shown.

1" x 4" x 10' (3.04 m of standard 1 x 4 lumber)

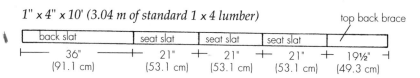

back slat	back slat	front leg	seat slat
36" (91.1 cm)	36" (91.1 cm)	24" (60.7 cm)	21" (53.1 cm)

1" x 4" x 10' (3.04 m of standard 1 x 4 lumber)

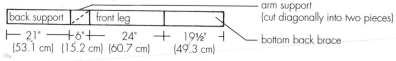

back slat	back slat	arm connector	seat slat
36" (91.1 cm)	36" (91.1 cm)	26" (65.8 cm)	21" (53.1 cm)

1" x 4" x 10' (3.04 m of standard 1 x 4 lumber)   top back brace

back slat	seat slat	seat slat	seat slat	
36" (91.1 cm)	21" (53.1 cm)	21" (53.1 cm)	21" (53.1 cm)	19½" (49.3 cm)

1" x 4" x 6' (1.82 m of standard 1 x 4 lumber)

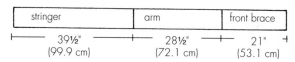

arm support
(cut diagonally into two pieces)

back support	front leg	
21" (53.1 cm)	6" (15.2 cm) 24" (60.7 cm)	19½" (49.3 cm)

bottom back brace

1" x 6" x 8' (2.43 m of standard 1 x 6 lumber)

stringer	arm	front brace
39½" (99.9 cm)	28½" (72.1 cm)	21" (53.1 cm)

1" x 6" x 6' (1.82 m of standard 1 x 6 lumber)

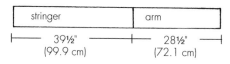

stringer	arm
39½" (99.9 cm)	28½" (72.1 cm)

2. Prepare the pieces. Sand all the pieces to remove any rough edges or imperfections in the wood. If you're going to paint the finished chair, prime the pieces now, before assembly.

3. Cut the front brace. The front brace, which fastens below the seat, is very visible on the finished chair. However, a simple curve can easily diminish the blockiness of this board. To curve the lower edge of the front brace, measure in 4" (10.1 cm) from each side and mark.

Tie a piece of string to a pencil. Using the string as a compass, draw a gently curving arc to 1" (2.5 cm) deep between these two points. Cut this arc with a jigsaw and smooth any rough edges with sandpaper.

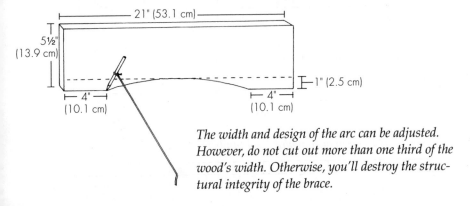

The width and design of the arc can be adjusted. However, do not cut out more than one third of the wood's width. Otherwise, you'll destroy the structural integrity of the brace.

4. Attach the front brace. Place the top edge of the front brace 15½" (39.2 cm) above the bottom of the front legs. Predrill, apply glue to adjoining surfaces, and screw through the front legs into the brace with three 2" screws evenly spaced and ⅜" (1 cm) in from the outside edge.

5. Cut the stringers. Cut the stringers to the dimensions shown.

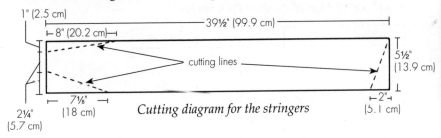

Cutting diagram for the stringers

6. Attach the stringers. Set the top edge of the stringers flush with the top edge of the front brace. Before screwing, ensure that the H-shape of the brace, legs, and stringers is level and that the tails of the stringers rest squarely on the ground. If you aren't working on a level surface, your chair won't sit properly.

Predrill, glue, and screw through the stringers into the front legs, three 1¼" screws per stringer, drilling from inside the chair (between the stringers). Space the three screws in a staggered or diagonal pattern. Then, in addition, screw through the legs into the stringers and through the front brace into the stringers to increase the strength of the joint.

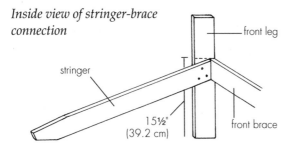

Inside view of stringer-brace connection

front leg

stringer

15½"
(39.2 cm)

front brace

7. Install the seat slats. Look carefully at each of your slats to determine which side should face up. If a board has knots or other imperfections, you can hide them simply by turning the board over.

Install the seat slats from front to back. Place the first slat between the legs, on top of the stringers and flush with the top edge of the front brace. Predrill two holes, one at each end of the slat, ⅜" (1 cm) in from the outside edge. Then glue and screw the slat into place. Be sure to countersink the 2" screws so that they don't protrude above the slat.

Predrill the next three slats and temporarily screw them into place with 2" screws; they will be flush with the outside edges of the stringers. Leave a ½" (1.3 cm) gap between the slats. (The gap will allow water to drain.) If the spacing is even, glue and screw the second, third, and fourth slats into place. Do not attach the fifth seat slat yet.

8. Install the back support. Measure 5" (12.7 cm) from the fourth slat and mark on each stringer. Predrill, glue, and screw the back support to the top of the stringers. The chair back will rest against this support.

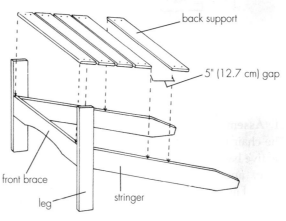

Placement of seat slats and back support

back support

5" (12.7 cm) gap

front brace

leg

stringer

9. Install the arm supports. Center the 5½" (13.9 cm) factory-cut edge of one of the arm-support triangles flush with the top of the leg. For the lower of two screw holes, angle the drill upward (so it won't penetrate the inner surface of the leg) and drill through the triangle into the leg with the pilot bit. Apply glue to adjoining surfaces, then screw the triangular arm support into the leg with two screws.

10. Cut the arms. With the two arms cut to length, measure down 2¾" (7 cm) along one factory-cut edge; mark and draw a line lightly across the face of the board from this point. Mark the center point of this line (at 2¾"). With this as the center of a circle, draw a semicircle with a 2¾" radius. The semicircle gives the arms a rounded edge. If you don't have a compass to do this, use a piece of string tied to a pencil. The string should measure 2¾" (7 cm) from the pencil point to its end. Tack the string at your 2¾" mark on the arm and, using it as a compass, scribe a semicircle along the edge of the arm.

Cut along this line with the jigsaw, and hand-sand, belt-sand, or palm-sand the sawed edges.

At the other end of each arm, measure in one direction 2¼" (5.7 cm) along the cut edge and 10" (25.3 cm) in a perpendicular direction along the factory-cut edge. Connect these points with a straightedge. Cut off this triangle with the circular saw or handsaw. The cut edge will be to the outside of the chair. Sand any rough edges.

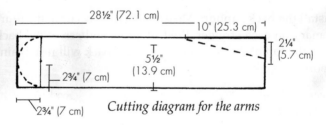

Cutting diagram for the arms

Set the arms aside until you've installed the chair back.

11. Assemble the chair back. The chair back is composed of the five back slats, the top back brace, and the bottom back brace. Lay the first back slat with its better side face down.

Quick Tip

Because the screws that connect the back braces to the slats will be visible from the back of the chair, establish a screwing pattern. You can space the screws either evenly in a horizontal line or in a staggered pattern.

On top of the slat place the top back brace, perpendicular to the slat and 6½" (16.4 cm) below the top of the slat. The cut edge of the brace should be flush with the factory-cut edge of the back slat. Predrill, glue, and screw through the brace into the slat with two 1¼" screws.

With the rafter's square, make sure that the brace is square to the slat.

Measure up from the bottom of the first back slat 3" (7.6 cm) and mark. Set the bottom back brace so that its lower edge is flush with this line. Predrill the brace and square it up before gluing and screwing it into the first slat.

Repeat this process with the fifth, or last, back slat, which you'll place at the opposite end of the braces. The edge of this slat should be flush with the cut ends of the braces. Predrill, glue, and screw together. Use with the rafter's square to make sure that all the angles are square and that the slats are square with each other.

Insert the remaining back slats with a ½" (1.3 cm) gap between them. If you have less (or more) than the required gap, divide the distance evenly among the slats.

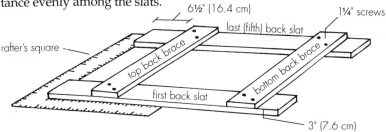

Attaching the braces to the first and last back slats

12. Cut an arc in the back. Turn the back over and, at the top, mark the center of the chair back; this should be at 9¾" (24.7 cm) from the edge. Draw a line 19½" (49.3 cm) long down the middle slat. Draw this line lightly, as the pencil marks will show, especially if you'll be varnishing or staining the chair.

Tie a piece of string to a pencil so that it measures 19½" (49.3 cm) from the pencil point to its end. Tack the string at your 19½" mark on the middle slat and, using the string as a compass, scribe an arc along the top ends of the five slats.

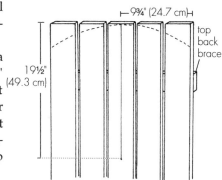

Scribing an arc on the back of the chair

Clamp the back to a stable work surface and cut along these lines with a jigsaw. Smooth the edges with a belt or palm sander; or you can hand-sand the edges.

13. Attach the back to the chair. Lift the back into the space between the stringers, with the bottom back brace sitting on the back support. Push the chair back tight against the back support. In order to adjust the angle, have a helper steady the chair back, or wedge a 2" x 4" board under the top back brace to temporarily secure the back.

In the space where the fifth seat slat will eventually go, predrill and screw a couple of screws through the back slats into the back support. These will act as pivot points while you adjust the angle of the chair back.

Set a T-bevel for 100 degrees and raise (or lower) the back accordingly; most people find this a comfortable angle. Sit, *tentatively*, in your chair (with your helper or the 2 x 4 supporting the back assembly) and adjust the angle until it feels right. Once you have determined the proper tilt, double-check that the bottom back brace is level and then screw through each slat into the back support. You also want to screw through the stringers into the first and last slats. Center the fifth seat slat between the fourth seat slat and the chair back; predrill, glue, and screw into place.

The chair back should now be self-supporting, but just to be sure, keep it braced until both the arms and the arm connector are finally in place.

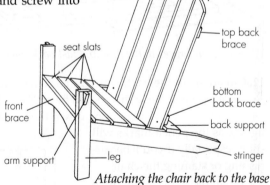

Attaching the chair back to the base

14. Install the arm connector. Rest the 4' (1.2 m) level on top of one of the front legs so that it extends beyond the first slat of the chair back. On the back slat, mark a level line. Save this angle on the T-bevel — you'll use it to cut pieces from the arm connector so that it can hold the arms level.

Rest the level on the second leg. When you have determined level, mark the angle on the last slat of the chair back.

Align the arm connector so that it butts against these angled lines. It will overhang the back slats by 3¼" (8.2 cm) on each side. Clamp the arm connector to the first and last slats. Before tightening the C-clamps, protect them with cardboard or wooden shims so they won't leave gouges in the wood. Check that the arm connector is level. With the clamps tightened, draw the angle that you saved on the T-bevel on each end of the arm connec-

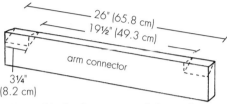

tor. Remove this triangular piece of wood with a hand- or jigsaw, a hammer, and a chisel. You can make the cut closest to the slats by angling your saw; the waste can then be easily removed with the hammer and chisel.

Use a chisel, a hammer, and the angle recorded by the T-bevel to cut triangular pieces from both ends of the arm connector.

With this triangular piece removed, the arms should sit tightly on the ends of the arm connector. Mark the placement of the arm connector on the back slats, then remove the C-clamps. Apply glue to the adjoining surfaces, reclamp, and screw the arm connector into the back slats.

15. Install the arms. To put the first arm in place, rest it on the arm connector and front leg. The curved end will sit on top of the leg with a ¾" (1.9 cm) overhang to the inside of the chair. The other end of the arm will be flush with the outside edge of the arm connector and tight against the slat.

Predrill, glue, and screw the arm into the leg, the triangular arm support, and the arm connector. Be sure the screws are countersunk.

Repeat this process with the second arm.

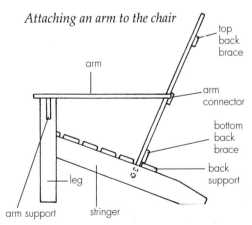

Attaching an arm to the chair

16. Add finishing touches. If you'll be painting your chair, fill the screw holes with a wood filler rated for exterior use. When the filler has dried, sand the rough surfaces. Sand off any pencil marks and finish the chair by staining, painting, or varnishing.

Making a Contoured Seat and Chair Back

You can curve the back of your Adirondack chair and chair seat for a more contoured fit. The curves can be of any arc within certain limits — if the arc is too severe, the slats won't fit side by side and the integrity of the stringers or back support will be compromised. Experiment with different curves until you find one that is especially comfortable and doesn't cut more than about an inch (2.5 cm) into the supporting pieces.

The Seat

1. Proceed with building the chair. Follow the instructions for building the Adirondack chair through step 4.

2. Cut and mark the stringer. Cut the stringer as shown for step 5, on page 8. At the top end (where the stringer meets the front brace), measure down along the factory-cut edge 3" (7.6 cm) and mark. This portion of the stringer will be covered by the chair leg. From the top of the stringer, measure down again and mark at 18¼" (46.2 cm); this mark designates the end of the last slat. The curve of the seat must occur between these two points.

3. Draw an arc on the stringer. Tie a piece of string to a pencil. Experiment with tacking the string at different marks and using different lengths of string as you practice drawing circles of different sizes on the stringer until you have an arc that you like. An arc with a shorter radius may create difficulty in seating the slats. If so, you can rip the slats in half lengthwise to accommodate a more severe curve, but the radius may still be too

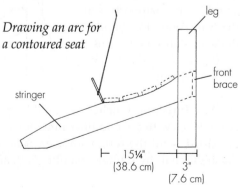

Drawing an arc for a contoured seat

leg

front brace

stringer

|— 15¼" —|
(38.6 cm)

3"
(7.6 cm)

severe for comfort and may compromise the structural integrity of the stringer. A curve that removes a width of 1" (2.5 cm) allows the slats to sit flat while providing a slight roll to the seat.

4. Cut the arc from the stringer. Once you've drawn the curve, cut along the line with a jigsaw, sand the rough edges, and use the first stringer as a pattern for cutting the second stringer.

5. Finish building. Attach the stringers as directed in step 6 (page 8), install the seat slats as directed in step 7 (page 9), and continue with the assembly as outlined in the chair directions.

The Back

To achieve a curved back is more complicated and requires the following adjustments:
- The back support and fifth slat should be of 1" x 6" stock, not 1" x 4".
- Although the arms will have the same cuts as described in the chair directions, they will be 30¾" (77.8 cm) long instead of 28½" (72.1 cm) long.
- Additional materials include two 20" (50.6 cm) lengths of 2" x 2" lumber for the vertical supports and six 2" (5.1 cm) screws.
- There is no bottom back brace; the slats are screwed directly into the back support.

1. Proceed with building the chair. Follow the instructions for building the Adirondack chair through step 10. When attaching the 1" x 6" back support in step 8, however, simply screw the piece temporarily into place.

2. Draw an arc on the back support. To create the curve of the back, measure in on the back support ¾" (1.9 cm) from both cut ends and mark. Tie a piece of string to a pencil and, using the string as a compass, draw circles of different radii between those marks until you have an arc that you like. Arcs with shorter radii may create difficulty seating the slats. If so, you can rip the slats in half lengthwise to accommodate a more severe curve, but the radius may still be too severe for comfort.

3. Cut the arc from the back support. Once you've chosen an arc, remove the back support and cut along the penciled line with the jigsaw set for an 80-degree angled cut. You can increase or decrease this angle, depending on whether you want the back to angle more than 100 degrees from seat to back. With cuts of more than 80 degrees, the back will be more vertical.

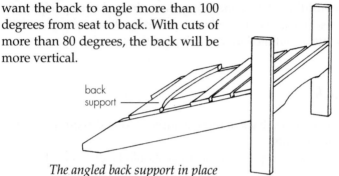

back support

The angled back support in place

4. Install the back support. Once the arc is cut, set the back support back on the chair; predrill, glue, and screw it into place.

5. Trace and cut the arc into the top back brace. Rip the top back brace to a width of 2¼" (5.7 cm). Using the curve of the back support as a template, draw the same curve on the top back brace and cut with your jigsaw set for a 70-degree cut.

6. Trace and cut the arc into the arm connector. Rip the arm connector to 2¼" (5.7 cm) wide. To translate the arc to the arm connector, measure in 3¼" (8.2 cm) from each end of the connector. Between these marks, position the arc of back support on the arm connector. Draw the arc and cut with your jigsaw set for a 70-degree angled cut.

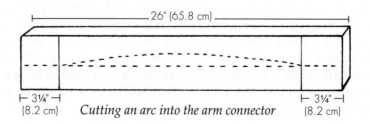

26" (65.8 cm)

3¼"
(8.2 cm)   *Cutting an arc into the arm connector*   3¼"
(8.2 cm)

7. Assemble the chair back. The contoured chair back is composed of the five back slats and the top back brace. Lay the top back brace on a level surface. Lay the first back slat on the top back brace, perpendicular to the slat, with its top edge 6½" (16.4 cm) above the top of the brace, with its better side face up, and with its factory-cut edge flush with the cut edge of the brace. Predrill, glue, and screw through the slat into the curved edge of the top brace with two screws.

With the rafter's square, make sure that the brace is square to the slat.

Repeat this process with the fifth, or last, back slat, which will be placed at the opposite end of the brace. The edge of the slat should be flush with the cut end of the brace. Predrill, glue, and screw together. Use the rafter square to make sure that all the angles are square and that the slats are square with each other.

Insert the remaining back slats with a ½" (1.3 cm) gap between them. If you have less (or more) than the required gap, divide the distance evenly among the slats. Again, check that the back slats are square with the brace and with each other.

8. Install the chair back. At the bottom end of the slats, measure up 3" (7.6 cm) and mark. The slats will be screwed into the back support ⅜" (1 cm) above this line.

With a helper, insert the slats and the top brace into the chair. Screw through the slats (two screws each) into the back support.

9. Trace the arc on the fifth slat. Before installing the arm connector, draw the inverse of its arc on the 1" x 6" fifth slat. Cut the slat with your jigsaw set for an 80-degree angle.

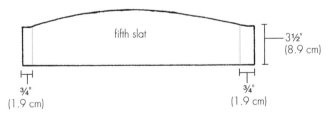

The inverse of the arc on the fifth slat

10. Install the arm connector and vertical supports. Set the arm connector in place by clamping it to the first and last slats. Check that it is level and projects 3¼" (8.2 cm) to each side beyond the slats, then drill, glue, and screw through the slats into the connector.

Two vertical supports will support the arm connector. Predrill, glue, and screw the vertical supports into the stringers with three 2" (5.1 cm) screws. With the level, check that they are plumb. Then screw through the arm connector into the supports.

11. Install the arms. To install the arms, follow the instructions in step 15 (page 13).

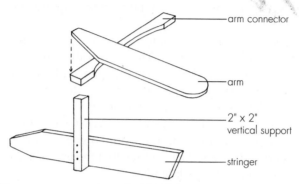

The arm connector is sandwiched between the vertical supports and the arms.

12. Install the fifth slat. The fifth slat fills the arced space left when the back of the chair is curved. Set the slat in place; predrill, glue, and screw into the stringers.

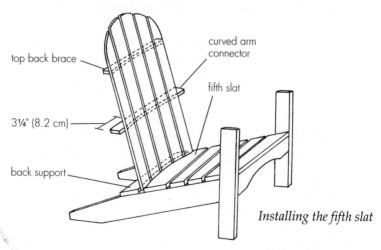

Installing the fifth slat

13. Add finishing touches. Finish the chair as instructed in step 16 (page 13).

The Footstool

An Adirondack chair isn't complete without a footstool. The stool is the same height as the chair, butts against the first chair slat, and slopes toward the ground.

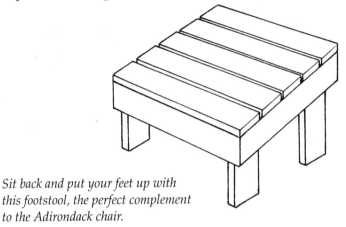

Sit back and put your feet up with this footstool, the perfect complement to the Adirondack chair.

Materials and Tools for the Footstool

Tools

Tape measure
Pencil
Circular saw or ripsaw
2' (61 cm) level
Carpenter's wood glue
Power drill with Phillips-head
    driver, or Phillips-head screw-
    driver
Drill bit for pilot holes
Sanding block, belt sander, or
    palm sander and assortment
    of sandpaper (coarse to fine)
Rafter's square

Fasteners

50 1⅝" (4.1 cm) stainless-steel
    drywall screws, **or**
#8 stainless-steel, brass, or
    galvanized wood screws

Lumber

2 10-foot (3 m) lengths of stan-
    dard 1" x 4" lumber

Cutting List for the Footstool

Quantity	Use	Dimensions	Length of Pieces
7	slats, front, and back of box	1" x 4"	21" (53.1 cm)
2	front legs	1" x 4"	15" (38 cm)
2	back legs	1" x 4"	10¾" (27.2 cm)
2	sides of box	1" x 4"	18" (45.5 cm)

1. Cut the pieces. Cut the lumber to the dimensions shown.

To cut the two front legs (these are the longer legs that will abut the seat of your Adirondack chair), measure along one factory edge to 15" (38 cm) and mark. Along the opposite edge, measure to 14" (35.4 cm) and mark. Draw a line between these points to get the proper angle. Cut the legs.

For the two back legs (the shorter legs), follow the same procedure for making the angled cut. Measure 10¾" (27.2 cm) along one edge and 9¾" (24.7 cm) along the other. Draw a line between these points. Then cut the legs.

Cut side pieces as illustrated, with angled cuts at both ends.

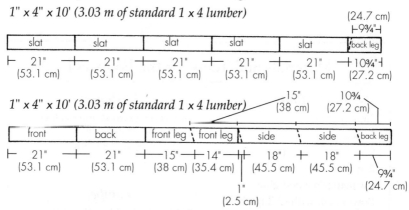

2. Prepare the pieces. Before assembly, sand the lumber lightly to remove any imperfections. Prime the pieces if you're planning to paint the finished footstool.

3. Join the sides to the legs. Place one back and one front leg on a flat surface. On top of these, align one side piece so that the top angles of the legs align with the side piece; the angled cuts of the side pieces should also line up with the outer factory-cut edges of the legs.

Predrill, glue, and screw together with two screws at either end. Stagger the screws in a diagonal pattern.

Repeat the same process with the other set of legs and the second side piece.

4. Assemble the legs. To connect the leg assemblies, predrill, glue, and screw the 21" (53.1 cm) long front piece to the legs with two 1¼" screws. Make sure the front piece is level. Then repeat the process with the back piece and leg assembly so that you have a completed box.

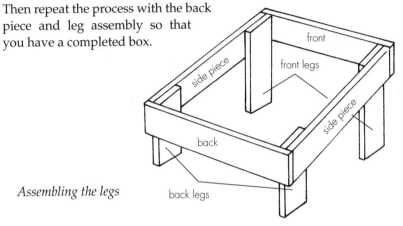

front

front legs

side piece

side piece

back

Assembling the legs

back legs

5. Test the stool. Set the footstool frame on a flat surface to ensure that all four legs contact the floor squarely.

6. Attach the slats. Align the edge of the first slat with the edge of the front piece. Predrill for three screws through the slat into the front and two screws at each end of the slat into the side pieces. Glue and screw into place using 2" screws. Repeat this process with the last slat at the opposite end of the footstool.

Evenly space the remaining slats; they should be ½" (1.3 cm) apart. Predrill, glue, and screw the slats with two 2" screws at each end of each slat.

7. Apply the finishing touches. Varnish, stain, or paint the stool. If you'll be painting it, fill the screw holes with a wood filler rated for exterior use. When the filler has dried, sand the rough surfaces, prime, and paint.

The Table

Whether or not you'll be building multiple chairs, a table makes a convenient addition to your array of Adirondack furniture.

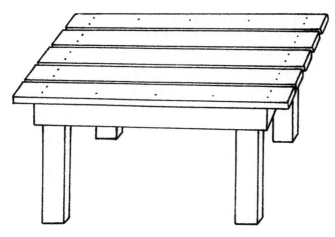

Match this Adirondack-style table with the Adirondack or Westport chair to create a wonderful display of rustic furniture.

Materials and Tools for the Table

Tools

Tape measure
Pencil
Circular saw or ripsaw
2' (61 cm) level
Carpenter's wood glue
Power drill with Phillips-head
driver, or Phillips-head screw-
driver
Drill bit for pilot holes
Sanding block, belt sander, or
palm sander and assortment
of sandpaper (coarse to fine)
Rafter's square

Fasteners

30 2" and thirty 1¼" stainless-
steel drywall screws, **or**
#8 stainless-steel, brass, or
galvanized wood screws

Lumber

1 6-foot (1.8 m) length of standard 1" x 4" lumber
1 8-foot (2.4 m) length of standard 1" x 4" lumber
1 10-foot (3 m) length of standard 1" x 4" lumber

Cutting List for the Table

Quantity	Use	Dimensions	Length of Pieces
5	slats	1" x 4"	26" (65.8 cm)
2	side braces	1" x 4"	20" (50.6 cm)
1	front brace	1" x 4"	17" (43 cm)
1	back brace	1" x 4"	17" (43 cm)
4	legs	1" x 4"	20" (50.8 cm)

1. Cut the pieces. Cut the lumber to the dimensions shown.

1" x 4" x 6' (1.82 m of standard 1 x 4 lumber)

slat	slat	side brace
26" (65.8 cm)	26" (65.8 cm)	20" (50.6 cm)

1" x 4" x 8' (2.43 m of standard 1 x 4 lumber)

slat	slat	slat	front brace
26" (65.8 cm)	26" (65.8 cm)	26" (65.8 cm)	17" (43 cm)

1" x 4" x 10' (3.03 m of standard 1 x 4 lumber)

side brace	leg	leg	leg	leg	back brace
20" (50.6 cm)	20" (50.6 cm)	20" (50.6 cm)	20" (50.6 cm)	20" (50.6 cm)	17" (43 cm)

2. Prepare the pieces. Sand all the pieces before assembly, and prime them all if you'll be painting your table.

3. Assemble the table box. The table box is composed of the front, back, and side braces. Place the front brace on its edge with the end of a side brace perpendicular to the cut end of the front brace. Check for square. Predrill, glue, and screw with two 2" screws through the side brace into the front brace.

Repeat the process at the other end of the side brace with the back brace.

Turn the assembly around, align the edges, check for square, and predrill, glue, and screw the other side brace into the front and back braces to complete a box.

4. Attach the legs. Tip the box so that the flat surface of one of the side braces rests on a level surface. Place the leg flat in the corner on top of the side brace; the cut end of the leg should be flush with the factory edge of the side brace. Predrill, glue, and install 1¼" screws into the side. Repeat the process at all four corners.

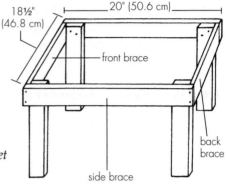

Check that when it's set upright, the box rests squarely on all four legs.

5. Attach the slats. The slats will run lengthwise. Align the first one to overhang both the front and back braces by 3" (7.6 cm) and the side brace by ½" (1.3 cm). Predrill, glue, and screw into the braces, being careful to mark the placement of the screws 3⅜" (8.5 cm) in from each cut end and ⅞" (2.2 cm) in from the factory edge. Repeat this process with the fifth slat along the opposite edge.

Evenly space the second, third, and fourth slats — there should be a gap of about ½" (1.3 cm) between them. Predrill, glue, and screw at both ends into the braces.

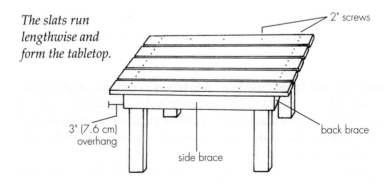

The slats run lengthwise and form the tabletop.

6. Apply the finishing touches. Apply sealer or varnish to all surfaces. If you'll be painting your table, first fill the screw holes with wood filler, and then sand and paint it.

The Westport Chair

The Adirondack chair has evolved into its current slatted design over time; Thomas Lee's original Westport chair was simpler than the modern-day Adirondack chair, with a smaller seat, much wider arms, fewer pieces, and wider boards.

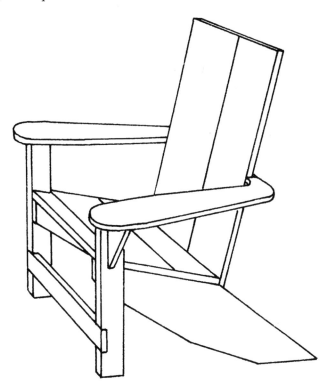

The precursor to the traditional Adirondack chair, the Westport chair was built more simply, using fewer pieces and wider boards.

Comfort Tip

If you'd like a rounded edge on the first slat — which can make your chair more comfortable — bevel its top edge with a plane, then sand for a smooth surface. This technique can also be applied to the Adirondack chair.

Materials and Tools for the Westport Chair

Tools

Tape measure

4' (1.2 m) level

Power drill with Phillips-head driver, or Phillips-head screwdriver

Drill bit for pilot holes

Circular saw or ripsaw

1" (2.5 cm) chisel

Rafter's square

Sanding block, palm sander, or belt sander with assortment of sandpaper (coarse to fine)

T-bevel

Hammer

Jigsaw

Handsaw

Pencil

Carpenter's wood glue

Fasteners

1 box of 1⅝" (4.1 cm) stainless-steel drywall screws, **or** #8 stainless-steel, brass, or galvanized wood screws (approximately 90 screws)

Lumber

1 10-foot (3 m) length of standard 1" x 4" lumber

1 2-foot (61 cm) length of standard 1" x 6" lumber

1 6-foot (1.8 m) length of standard 1" x 8" lumber

1 8-foot (2.4 m) length of standard 1" x 10" lumber

1 10-foot (3 m) length of standard 1" x 10" lumber

Cutting List for the Westport Chair

Quantity	Use	Dimensions	Length of Pieces
2	arms	1" x 10"	32½" (82.2 cm)
1	back slat	1" x 10"	39¼" (99.3 cm)
2	stringers	1" x 10"	33½" (84.8 cm)
1	chair slat	1" x 10"	22" (55.7 cm)
1	back slat	1" x 8"	39¼" (99.3 cm)
1	arm support	1" x 8"	12" (30.4 m)
1	chair slat	1" x 6"	22" (55.7 cm)
1	chair slat	1" x 4"	18" (45.5 cm)
1	arm connector	1" x 4"	31½" (79.7 cm)
2	legs	1" x 4"	24" (60.7 cm)
1	front brace	1" x 4"	19½" (49.3 cm)

Note: I used the widest precut boards available to keep the feel of the Westport chair, but it doesn't make for an efficient use of wood. If you wish to rip boards to fit, adjust your dimensions accordingly.

1. Cut the pieces. Cut the lumber to the dimensions shown.

1" x 10" x 10' (3.03 m of standard 1 x 10 lumber)

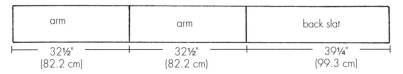

arm	arm	back slat
32½"	32½"	39¼"
(82.2 cm)	(82.2 cm)	(99.3 cm)

1" x 10" x 8' (2.43 m of standard 1 x 10 lumber)

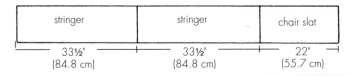

stringer	stringer	chair slat
33½"	33½"	22"
(84.8 cm)	(84.8 cm)	(55.7 cm)

1" x 8" x 6' (1.82 m of standard 1 x 8 lumber)

arm support	back slat
12"	39¼"
(30.4 cm)	(99.3 cm)

1" x 6" x 2' (60 cm of standard 1 x 6 lumber)

chair slat
22"
(55.7 cm)

1" x 4" x 10' (3.03 m of standard 1 x 4 lumber)

leg	leg	front brace	arm connector	chair slat
24"	24"	19½"	31½"	18"
(60.7 cm)	(60.7 cm)	(49.3 cm)	(79.7 cm)	(45.5 cm)

2. Cut a dado in the front leg for the front brace. To cut a dado, or groove, for the front brace, measure up 3" (7.6 cm) from the bottom of the front leg and draw a line on the face of the leg with your rafter's square. Make a second measurement at 6½" (16.4 cm) and draw a second line on the face of the leg with your rafter's square. Measure in ¾" (1.9 cm) along each line, mark, and connect the points.

Place the leg in a vise or clamp it to a sturdy surface. Remove this ¾" x 3½" (1.9 x 8.9 cm) block by hand sawing along both lines and once or twice between these lines. The saw should penetrate the wood to a depth of only ¾". Chisel away the waste to gauge your lines.

Repeat the process on the second leg and set both legs aside.

Cutting a dado for the front brace

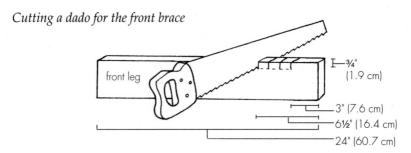

3. Cut the stringers to size. Cut each stringer as shown. For the first angled cut, measure 2¾" (7 cm) along one factory edge. Draw a diagonal line from that point to the opposite corner of the board (point A). Cut with a circular saw.

Along the other cut end of the stringer, measure up 3" (7.6 cm) and mark (point B). From this point, draw a line that is 10½" (26.6 cm) long when it hits the factory edge. Cut along this line with the circular saw.

At the 10½" (26.6 cm) mark, measure 8" (20.2 cm) along the factory edge and mark (point C). From point A on the stringer, measure in 3⅜" (8.5 cm) and mark (point D). Connect points C and D, and cut along this line. From point A, measure 19¼" (48.7 cm) and mark. Draw a line from this mark to point B and cut with your saw.

Use this stringer as a pattern for your second stringer.

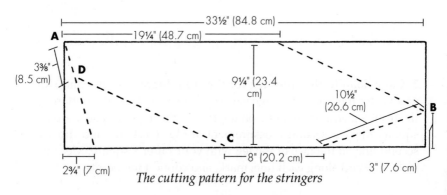

The cutting pattern for the stringers

4. Assemble the legs and stringers. Place one of the legs on a flat surface. Lay one stringer on top so that its front cut edge aligns with the factory-cut edge of the leg. The bottom edge of the stringer will be 12" (30.4 cm) above the bottom of the chair leg. The dado cut for the front brace should face away from the tail of the stringer. Predrill, glue, and screw through the stringer into the leg, then through the leg into the stringer. Repeat this procedure with the second leg and second stringer. Stand each assembly on a level surface to ensure that the legs and stringers sit squarely on the ground.

5. Install the seat slats. Install the seat slats from front to back without any space between them. The outside front edge of the first seat slat should be beveled with a plane and smoothed with sandpaper. The first seat slat sits on top of stringers and between the two vertical legs. Predrill, glue, and screw the slat into the stringers with two screws at each end of the slat.

The second seat slat will fit tightly against the legs and the first slat; it will overhang the stringers by 1¼" (3.2 cm) on each side. Predrill, glue, and drill with three screws at both ends.

Cut one factory-cut edge of the third seat slat at a 78-degree bevel. The chair back slats will sit flush against this angle. Predrill, glue, and screw the beveled slat into the stringer with three screws evenly spaced at each end.

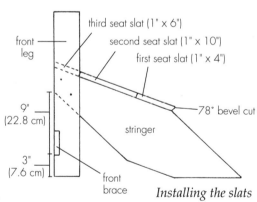

Installing the slats

6. Attach the back slats. On each of the two back slats, measure up 10" (25.3 cm) and mark. Predrill, glue, and screw the slats into the beveled third seat slat ⅜" (1 cm) below your marks. Also screw through the stringers into the back slat tails with two screws.

7. Attach the front brace. Fit the front brace into each of the dado cuts. It should be flush with the outside edge of the legs. Predrill, glue, and screw with two screws. Check that the brace is level.

8. Cut the arms. Cut the curves for the arms as shown. Carefully sand all surfaces with a sanding block or a palm or belt sander. Set aside.

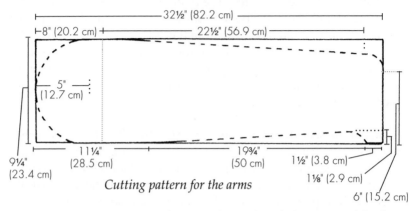

Cutting pattern for the arms

9. Cut the arm connector. Cut a 78-degree bevel along one of the factory-cut edges of the arm connector. Cut both ends of the arm connector to a 45-degree angle. Test your cuts by holding the arm connector against the middle of the chair back. The arms will sit level on the arm connector; the 45-degree angled cuts are to round off the arm/back/connector assembly. Once the chair is completed, sand this connection for a smooth surface.

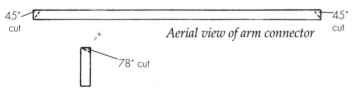

Aerial view of arm connector

Side view of arm connector

10. Attach the arm connector. Have a helper hold the angled chair back while you assemble the arms and arm connector. Set the 4' (1.2 m) level on one of the legs and mark a level line on the first slat. Repeat the process with the level on the second leg and mark a level line on the last slat.

Align the arm connector with these marks; the angles should match. The connector will extend 7¼" (18.3 cm) beyond the slats. Check that the arm connector is level, then clamp the connector to the slats. Predrill, glue, and screw through the slats into the arm connector.

11. Attach the arms. Rest the ends of the arms flush with the outside edge of the arm connector. The arms will overhang in front of the legs — approximately 7⅛" (18.1 cm) — but should be flush with the inner face of the leg. Predrill, glue, and screw together.

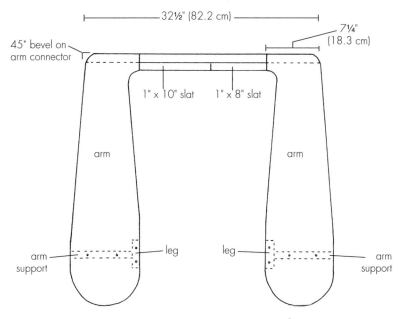

Aerial view of arm connector and arms

12. Attach the arm supports. Cut a 12" (30.3 cm) piece of 1" x 8" diagonally for the two arm supports. Sand the saw kerfs.

Place the 12" (30.3 cm) factory-cut edge of one of the triangles flush with the top of the leg and set back 1" from the outside (front) edge of the leg. Predrill, glue, and screw into the leg (check that the screw hasn't penetrated the inner surface of the leg; if it has, angle your drill upward and predrill again). Then screw the arm into the arm support with two screws; then through the leg into the arm support with two screws. Repeat the process for the second leg.

13. Apply the finishing touches. Remove pencil marks and sand all surfaces. Finish the chair by staining, varnishing, or painting.

Other Storey Titles You Will Enjoy

The Backyard Homestead Book of
Building Projects by Spike Carlsen
More than 75 useful structures to make your backyard
more productive, from cold frames and workbenches,
to chicken coops and flowerpot smokers.

How to Build a Fence by Jeff Beneke
Use this beginner-friendly, compact guide to build
a fence suited to your needs. Step-by-step instructions
cover the most popular basic styles of fence, including
picket, vertical board, and chain-link.

Making Bent Willow Furniture
by Brenda & Brian Cameron
Step-by-step instructions to make traditional willow
furniture for your home, porch, yard, and garden.

Making Bentwood Trellis, Arbors,
Gates & Fences by Jim Long
A thorough guide to collecting limbs from
native trees, then using them to craft a variety
of designs for the garden.

Reinventing the Chicken Coop
by Kevin McElroy & Matthew Wolpe
Complete plans for 14 stylish, sustainable, and
fully functional coops for every level of builder.

Woodworking FAQ by Spike Carlsen
Practical answers to common woodworking questions,
plus insider tips on how to be successful in every project.

Join the conversation. Share your experience with this book,
learn more about Storey Publishing's authors, and read
original essays and book excerpts at storey.com.
Look for our books wherever quality books are sold or by calling 800-441-5700.